COUNTRY EXPLORERS

A Visit to

SOUTH KOREA

by John Wood

BEARPORT PUBLISHING

Minneapolis, Minnesota

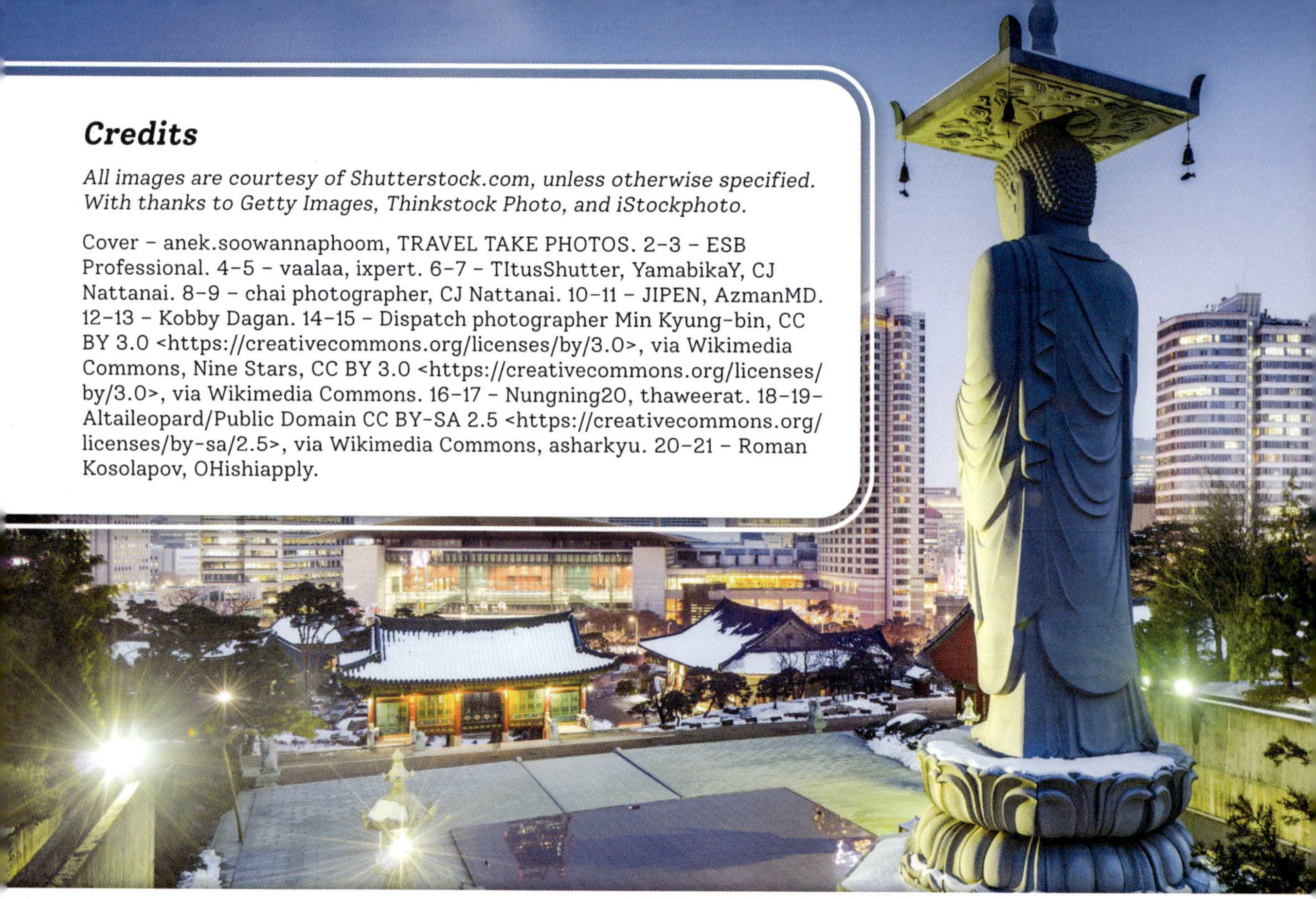

Credits

All images are courtesy of Shutterstock.com, unless otherwise specified. With thanks to Getty Images, Thinkstock Photo, and iStockphoto.

Cover – anek.soowannaphoom, TRAVEL TAKE PHOTOS. 2–3 – ESB Professional. 4–5 – vaalaa, ixpert. 6–7 – TItusShutter, YamabikaY, CJ Nattanai. 8–9 – chai photographer, CJ Nattanai. 10–11 – JIPEN, AzmanMD. 12–13 – Kobby Dagan. 14–15 – Dispatch photographer Min Kyung-bin, CC BY 3.0 <https://creativecommons.org/licenses/by/3.0>, via Wikimedia Commons, Nine Stars, CC BY 3.0 <https://creativecommons.org/licenses/by/3.0>, via Wikimedia Commons. 16–17 – Nungning20, thaweerat. 18–19–Altaileopard/Public Domain CC BY-SA 2.5 <https://creativecommons.org/licenses/by-sa/2.5>, via Wikimedia Commons, asharkyu. 20–21 – Roman Kosolapov, OHishiapply.

Library of Congress Cataloging-in-Publication Data is available at www.loc.gov or upon request from the publisher.

ISBN: 979-8-88509-045-2 (hardcover)
ISBN: 979-8-88509-056-8 (paperback)
ISBN: 979-8-88509-067-4 (ebook)

For more information, write to Bearport Publishing, 5357 Penn Avenue South, Minneapolis, MN 55419. Printed in the United States of America.

CONTENTS

COUNTRY TO COUNTRY

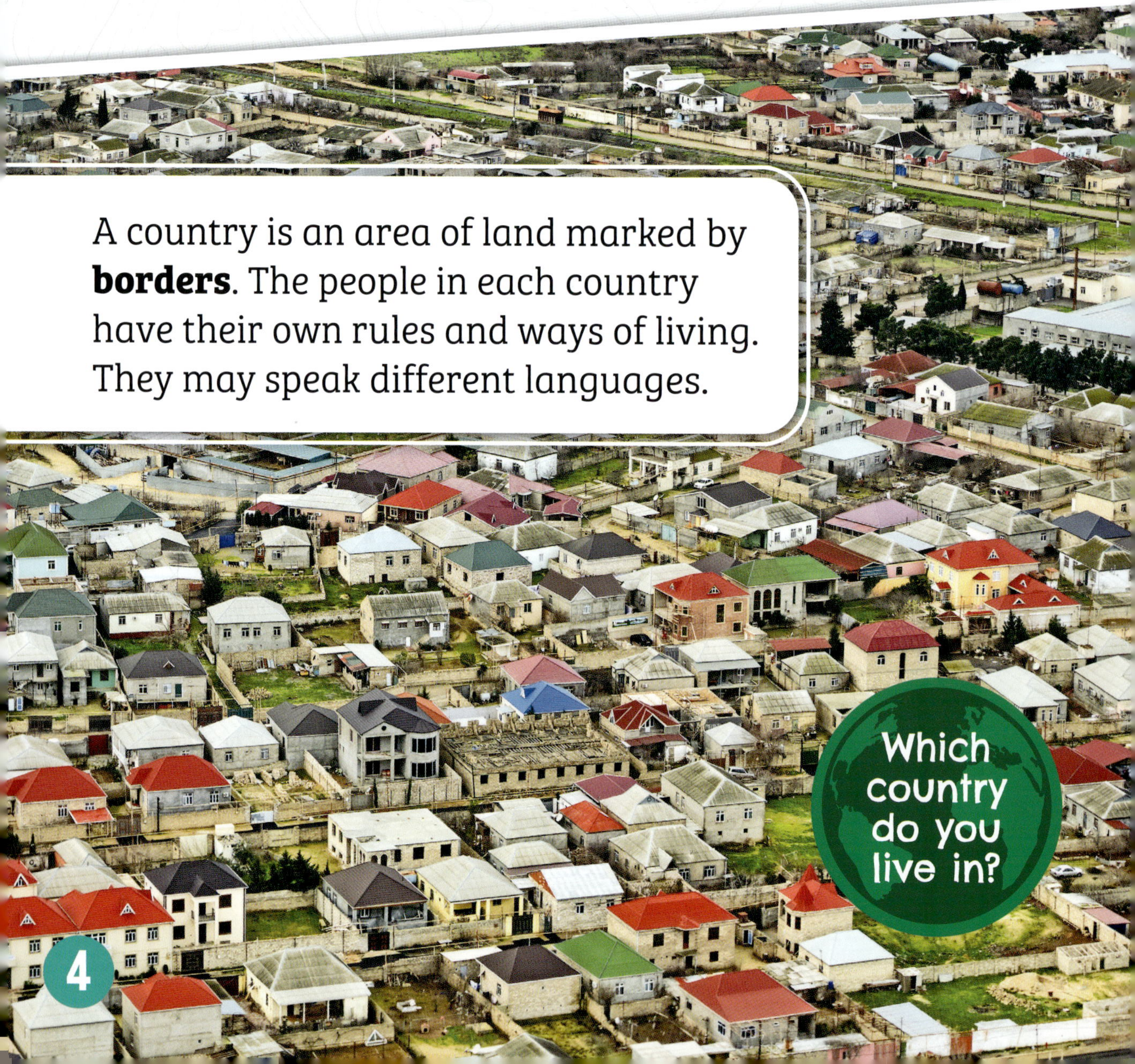

A country is an area of land marked by **borders**. The people in each country have their own rules and ways of living. They may speak different languages.

Which country do you live in?

Each country around the world has its own interesting things to see and do. Let's take a trip to visit a country and learn more!

Have you ever visited another country?

TODAY'S TRIP IS TO SOUTH KOREA!

South Korea is a country in the **continent** of Asia.

FACT FILE

Capital city: Seoul
Main language: Korean
Currency: Won
Flag:

Currency is the type of money that is used in a country.

SEOUL

We'll start our trip in South Korea's capital city, Seoul. The city has a lot of tall **skyscrapers**, but one of the highest points is Seoul Tower. It was built on Namsan Mountain to send **radio waves** to the city. But now, many people visit the tower for fun, too!

Bukchon Hanok Village is an area of Seoul full of **traditional** Korean houses called *hanoks*. Many of these houses are about 600 years old.

JEJU ISLAND

Next, we'll visit Jeju Island, near the southern tip of the country. It is home to Hallasan, South Korea's biggest mountain. Hallasan is a **volcano**.

Jeju Island has some of the largest **lava** tubes in the world. These tunnels and caves once had lava flowing through them. Today, they form an underground maze.

JINJU NAMGANG YUDEUNG FESTIVAL

Time for a celebration! During Jinju Namgang Yudeung Festival, people make lanterns and let them float along the Namgang River. There are also fireworks and **performances**.

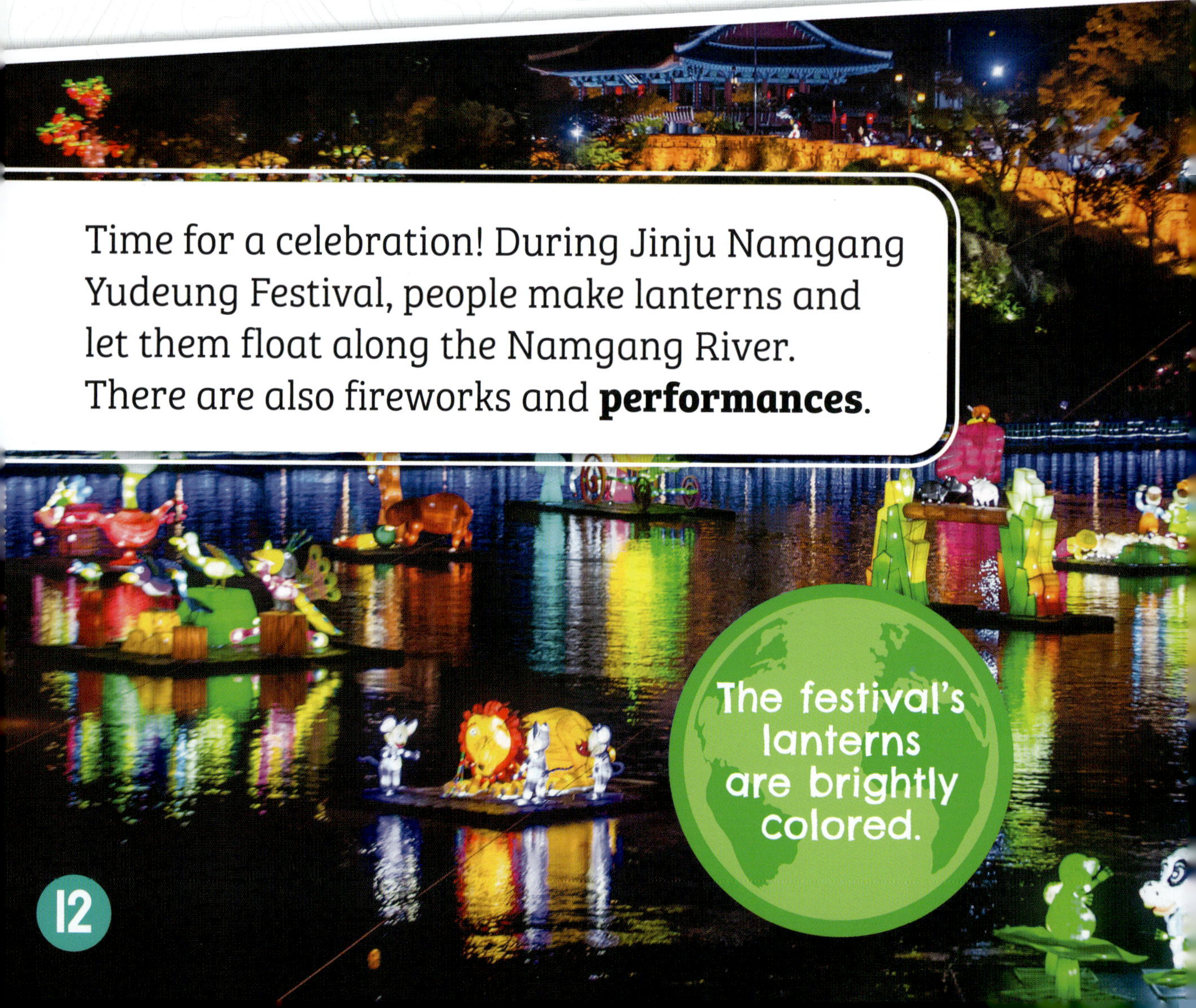

The festival's lanterns are brightly colored.

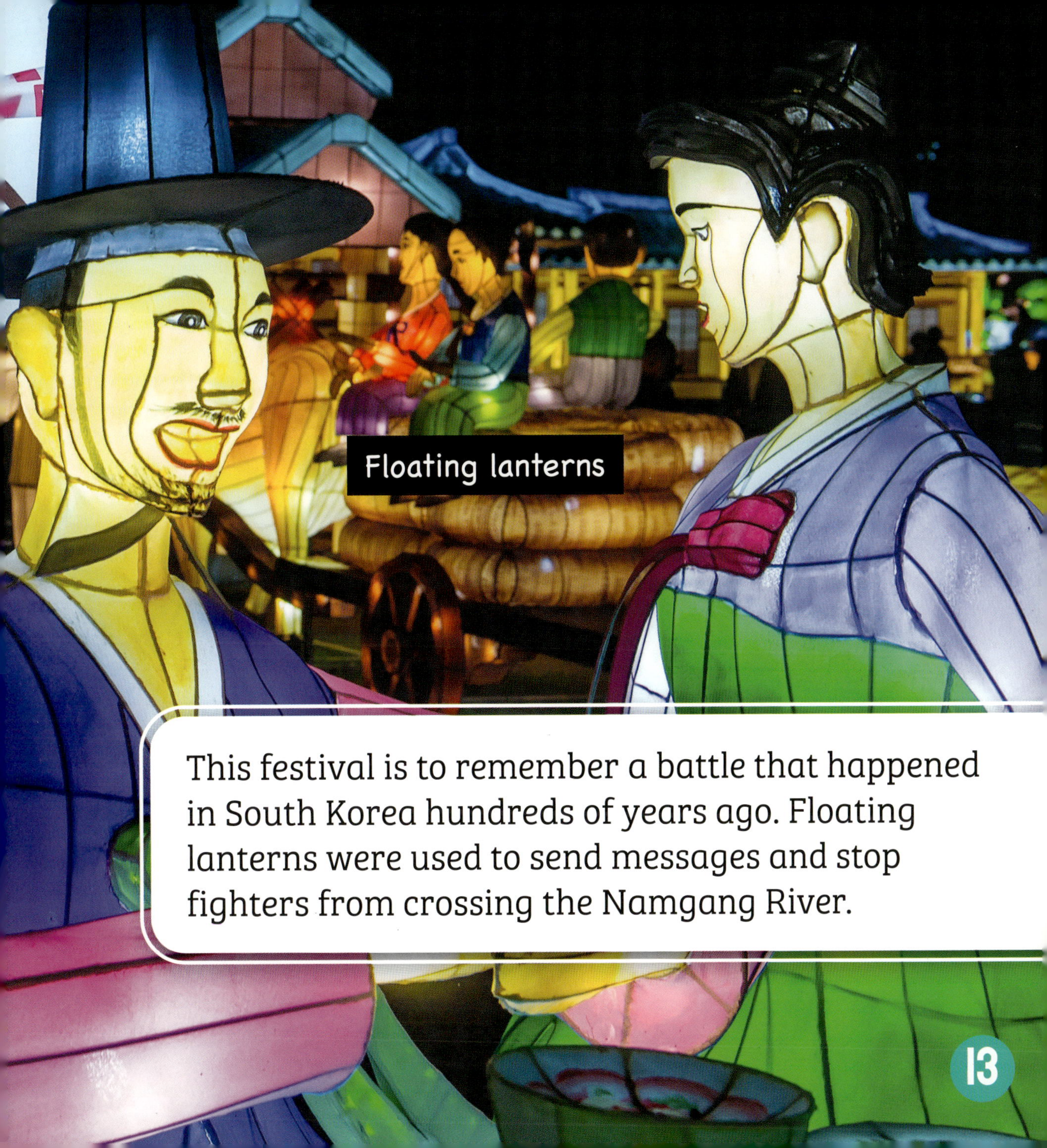

Floating lanterns

This festival is to remember a battle that happened in South Korea hundreds of years ago. Floating lanterns were used to send messages and stop fighters from crossing the Namgang River.

K-POP

South Korea is also the home of K-pop. This type of music has become popular around the world. K-pop is full of catchy songs and fun **dance routines**.

K-pop singers often make music videos.

K-pop is usually performed by groups. The singers work very hard to learn all their songs and dances.

FOOD

Feeling hungry? Let's grab something to eat! Kimchi is one of the most famous foods from South Korea. It is made from cabbage and spices.

Kimchi

Bibimbap is another famous South Korean food. It is a bowl of rice with vegetables and sauce on top. The dish often includes meat and an egg, too.

People usually mix up their bibimbap before eating it.

ANIMALS

Outside of South Korea's cities, we can meet some animals, such as the water deer. Water deer are small deer with no antlers. However, they do have fangs!

Some people call these animals vampire deer because of their fangs.

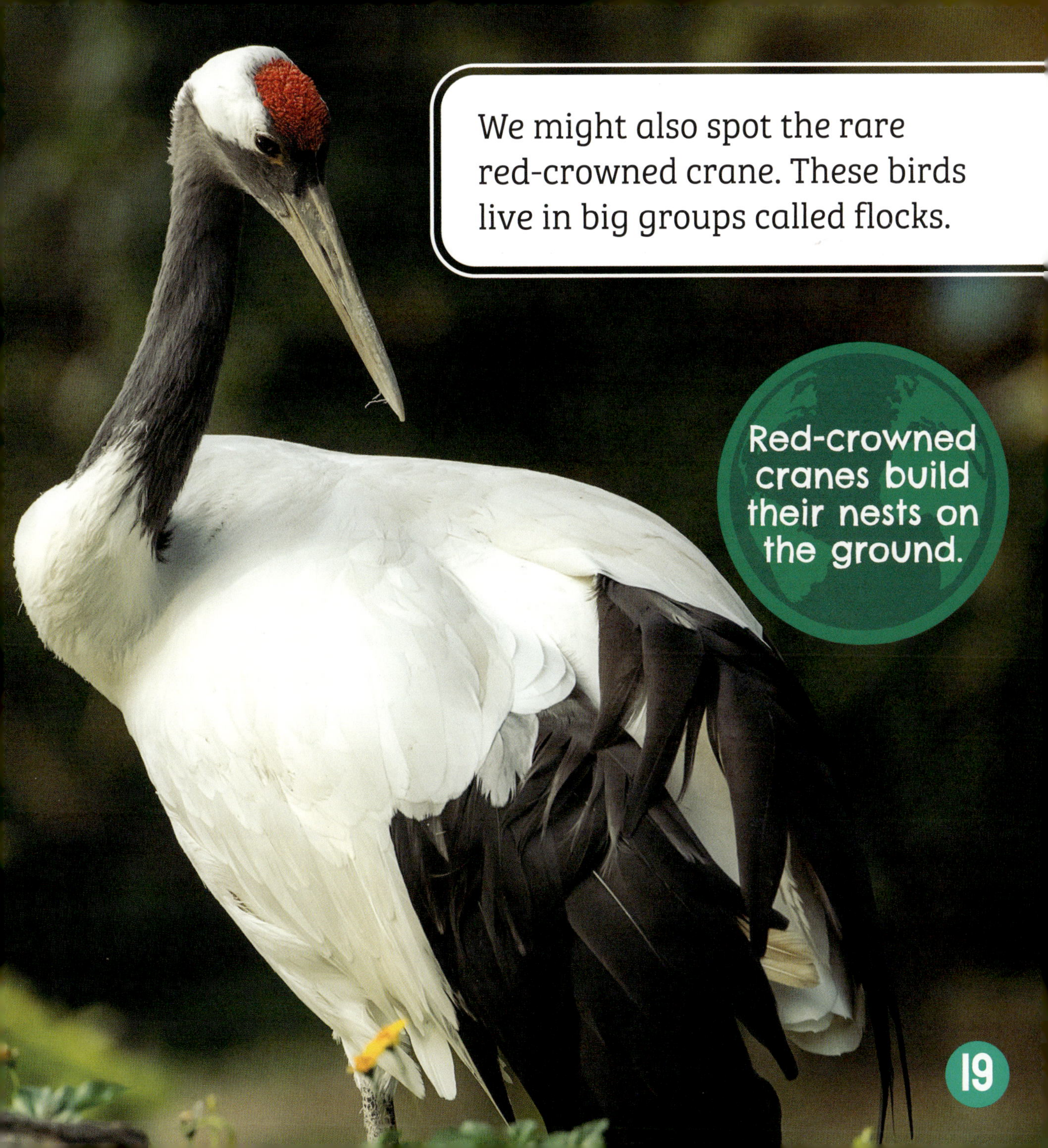

We might also spot the rare red-crowned crane. These birds live in big groups called flocks.

Red-crowned cranes build their nests on the ground.

eSPORTS

Next, we'll go watch some video games! When video games are played in a **competitive** way, they are called eSports. Many people say eSport competitions started in South Korea. They are often held in huge stadiums.

South Korea offers many ways for gamers to become better at eSports. There are lots of places where people can play video games together. The country even has video game schools.

Many eSport competitions are shown on TV.

BEFORE YOU GO

We can't forget to see Gyeongbokgung Palace! It was first built in 1395. After it was destroyed by a fire, the palace was rebuilt in the 1860s.

Gyeongbokgung Palace is the biggest of five palaces in Seoul.

Finally, let's visit the Huwon Secret Garden, which is behind Changdeokgung Palace in Seoul. Many of the garden's beautiful trees are more than 300 years old.

What have you learned about South Korea on this trip?

GLOSSARY

borders lines that show where one place ends and another begins

competitive related to people or teams trying to do something better than others

continent one of the world's seven large land masses

dance routines dance moves that are put together in a certain order

lava hot, flowing melted rock

performances shows for people to watch

radio waves invisible signals sent through the air to make radios and TVs work

skyscrapers tall buildings found in cities

traditional relating to something that a group of people has done for many years

volcano a mountain that can erupt to let out lava

INDEX